Caitlin Clark

IOWA
22
Wilson

Caitlin Clark

Sarah Gilbert

Living in THE SPOTLIGHT

CREATIVE EDUCATION
CREATIVE PAPERBACKS

NCAA
B1G
Iowa
22

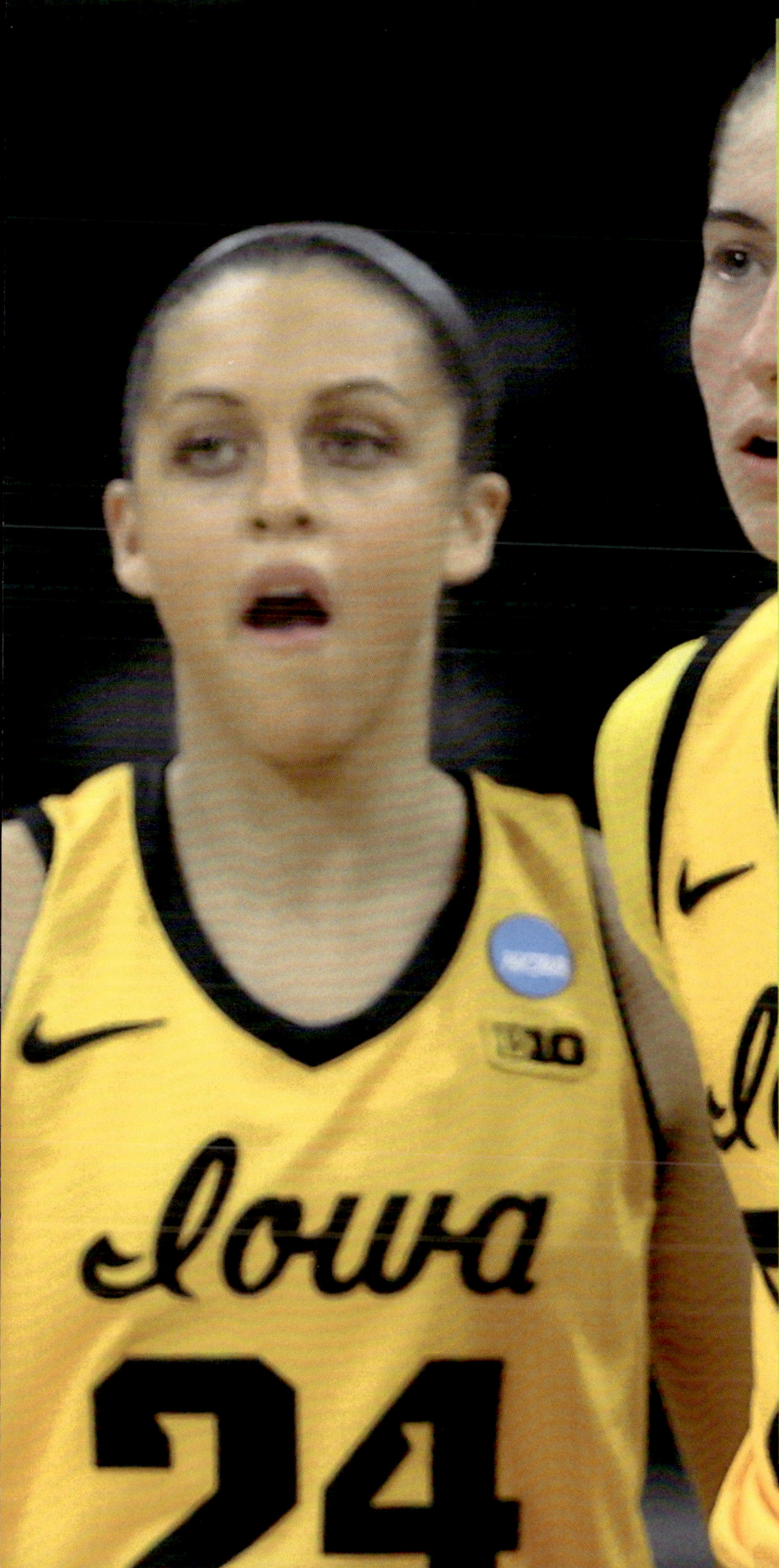

Published by Creative Education and Creative Paperbacks
P.O. Box 227, Mankato, Minnesota 56002
Creative Education and Creative Paperbacks are imprints
of The Creative Company
www.thecreativecompany.us

Book design by Wyeth Morgan (www.bluedes.com)
Art direction by Tom Morgan

Images by Associated Press/Eyepix/NurPhoto, cover; Getty Images/ANGELA WEISS, 43, Andy Lyons, 2, Ben Solomon, 30, Brian Spurlock/Icon Sportswire, 20, C. Morgan Engel, 19, 26, Carmen Mandato, 13, Cora Veltman/Sportico, 37, Greg Nelson, 9, Jeffrey Brown/Icon Sportswire, 23, Justin Tafoya, 17, Luke Lu/ Diamond Images, 10, Matthew Holst, 35, 46, Rebecca Gratz, 4–5, 29, Roy Rochlin, 45; Wikimedia Commons/JazzyJoeyD, 33, John Mac, CC BY-SA 2.0, cover, 6–7, 14, 25, 38, 41, 44

Library of Congress Cataloging-in-Publication Data
Names: Gilbert, Sarah, 1967- author
Title: Caitlin Clark / by Sara Gilbert.
Description: Mankato, Minnesota : Creative Education and Creative Paperbacks, [2026] | Series: Living in the spotlight | Includes bibliographical references and index. | Audience: Ages 10-14 | Audience: Grades 7-9 | Summary: "Get to know WNBA basketball star Caitlin Clark in this sports biography that showcases her athletic achievements in high school and with the Indiana Fever, personal challenges, and off-court ventures. Written for middle-grade readers, it includes table of contents, sidebars, glossary, resources, and index"— Provided by publisher.
Identifiers: LCCN 2025021190 (print) | LCCN 2025021191 (ebook) | ISBN 9798895811276 library binding | ISBN 9798896800804 paperback | ISBN 9798895812532 ebook
Subjects: LCSH: Clark, Caitlin, 2002—-Juvenile literature | Iowa Hawkeyes (Women's basketball team)—History | Women's National Basketball Association—Juvenile literature | Women basketball players—United States—Biography—Juvenile literature | Basketball players—United States—Biography—Juvenile literature | Women college athletes—Biography—Juvenile literature | Basketball for women—Records—United States—Juvenile literature | LCGFT: Biographies
Classification: LCC GV884.C554 G55 2026 (print) | LCC GV884. C554 (ebook) | DDC 796.323082092—dc23/eng/20250725
LC record available at https://lccn.loc.gov/2025021190
LC ebook record available at https://lccn.loc.gov/2025021191

Printed in the United States

FEVER
22
salesforce
AT&T

CONTENTS

Introduction

Number 22 has the ball. Her black-and-gold high-top sneakers flash as she flies up the court, dribbling easily as she runs. Her long, dark ponytail bounces in time with her feet, making every movement look practiced and graceful. Her teammates position themselves around her, ready to accept a pass or cut off an incoming opponent. A defender darts around her, trying to guess where she'll go next and when she'll stop to shoot. Suddenly, still more than 25 feet (7.6 meters) away from the hoop, number 22 slows her pace. She quickly plants her feet on the hardwood and almost immediately lifts them both up again in a low jump, her 6-foot (1.8-meter) frame easily stretching up as her arms arc over her head. She releases the basketball and watches as it soars in a perfect **parabola** toward the hoop. It gently hits the rim and swooshes through the net. As the ball drops to the floor, she bounces lightly on her toes as she runs backward, her fists clenched at her sides and her mouth curved into a smile. But that smile is quickly replaced by the serious game face for which number 22 is known. She's already moved on to the next play of the game, her attention focused on her opponents and the movement of the ball up the court. As she positions herself to defend, the crowd is still cheering and the announcers are sharing the news throughout the arena: another three-pointer for Caitlin Clark!

SOUTH CAROLINA
12
IOWA
22
IOWA
20
Wilson

Caitlin Clark plays for the All Iowa Attack team in April of 2017.

CHAPTER ONE:

Always Athletic

Caitlin Clark was just four years old when her older brother Blake was learning to ride his bike. Her parents were helping Blake figure out how to balance when Clark came outside and grabbed a bike, too. She quickly started zipping around the yard of their home.

That was one of the first clues Brent Clark and Anne Nizze-Clark had that their daughter had natural athletic abilities. But it didn't come as a complete surprise, given Clark's family history. Her grandfather was the football coach at Dowling Catholic High School in West Des Moines, Iowa, where her Aunt Kathy also played basketball. Her father was a star athlete in high school and went on to play both basketball and baseball at Simpson College in Indianola, Iowa. And her bothers—Blake, who is older, and Collin, who is younger—also showed an early interest in sports and were her earliest teammates and opponents.

Clark's abilities became more apparent when she started playing youth recreational sports. She played on soccer, softball, and volleyball teams as a child. She learned tennis and golf. And, at the age of five, she signed up to join her first basketball team.

There weren't any youth basketball teams for girls near the Clark's home in West Des Moines. So Clark played on a boy's team, and her father volunteered to help coach. During one game, he pulled her off the court when she got upset about the way an opponent was playing. He was bigger than her, and she didn't think he was playing fairly. Clark's father sat her on the bench and told her that she could go back in when she calmed down. Clark quickly stopped crying—and when she went back out, she preceded to fiercely block and even push that player out of bounds.

By the time she was in second grade, Clark was helping her **Amateur** Athletic Union (AAU) boy's team win the state **tournament**. In fact, she was so important to the team's success that her father overheard parents from the opposing team complain that girls shouldn't be allowed to play on the boy's team.

Although Clark loved all the sports she played, it quickly became clear that she had two favorites: soccer and basketball. It also became clear to those watching her play that she had special skills. She could dribble well almost immediately and developed great anticipation and court vision even in grade school. She worked hard in practices and was a fierce competitor in every game.

By the time she started high school at Dowling Catholic, Clark was nationally known as the star of her AAU team, the All Iowa Attack. She was so well known that Kristen Meyer, who had just started coaching the girl's basketball team at Dowling, was receiving calls

Clark goes in for the shot, determined to make it despite the intense defense surrounding her.

HAWKEYES
22
11

ZOOM IN: COOKIE MONSTER

Clark's favorite postgame snack was a plate of warm chocolate chip cookies, which were often waiting for her at the Dowling Catholic High School concession stand. Teammates remember that she made a beeline to the concession stand as soon as the game was over—although she usually stopped to say hi to her family first. But Clark's love of cookies wasn't limited to after games. She often grabbed a handful before heading to practice or a film session and once texted Coach Meyer to say she and her teammates would be late because they were waiting for their cookies to bake.

from college coaches asking about Clark. "They were predicting her to be top level," Meyer told reporters in Des Moines. "Some of them said that, even as a freshman in high school, she could've played on their Division I team."

Instead, she stepped right into a starting role on the Dowling Catholic **varsity** team. Coach Meyer recognized that Clark had an advanced understanding of the game and that she could pull off plays—like a behind-the-back pass to set up a scoring play—that others couldn't. Clark also prepared more than other players. She watched film from opposing teams on her own and coordinated extra shooting practices with her teammates. And she would always arrive first to get more shots in herself.

In her first year playing for the Dowling Catholic Maroons, Clark helped the team get to the first round of the Class 5A state tournament. As a **point guard**, she averaged 15.3 points, 4.7 assists and 2.3 steals per game, and the team put together a 19–5 record. As a sophomore, Clark averaged more than 27 points a game and ranked second in the country in scoring. The Maroons posted 20 wins and just four losses in the regular season and made it all the way to the quarterfinals in the state tournament. The postseason accolades started piling up. Clark was named the Central Iowa Metro League Player of the Year by *The Des Moines Register* and first-team Class 5A All State by the Iowa Print Sports Writers Association.

Clark's advanced playing ability sometimes led to frustration on the court. Coach Meyer had to show her video of her physical reactions to dropped passes or other misplays. Clark's body language—

throwing her arms in the air, for example, or clapping loudly—may have suggested that she had a bad attitude. Coach Meyer knew it was because she set high standards for herself and that she struggled when other players didn't take the game as seriously, but she didn't want college coaches to be concerned.

Colleges had started pursuing Clark while she was still in middle school. She received her first letter of interest from Missouri State before she started seventh grade. By the time she was a sophomore, ESPN had ranked her as the top player in her class and several more colleges had started actively recruiting her. The attention ramped up even more during her junior year, when she posted 60 points in one game and then broke the state single-game record for three-pointers with 13. She averaged 32.6 points, 6.8 rebounds, 3.6 assists and 2.3 steals per game, and was once again lauded with several state-wide awards at the end of the season.

Before the start of her senior season, Clark had verbally committed to playing college basketball at Notre Dame. But by late fall, she had reconsidered that decision. On November 19, 2019, she announced that she would play for the University of Iowa instead. She liked Iowa's coach, Lisa Bluder, and appreciated the way the team played. She knew that there was an opportunity to make an impact right away. And she wanted to help her home state team make it back to the Final Four for the first time since 1993 and win a national championship.

ZOOM IN: THE COLLEGE DECISION

Clark's dream as a young basketball player was to play for the University of Connecticut—also known as UConn. Although she was recruited to play at several colleges, including Iowa State, Texas, Oregon, and Oregon State, no scholarship offer came from UConn. Only after she had decided on Iowa and started her college career there did the reason for that come to light: UConn had already recruited Paige Bueckers, a talented guard from Hopkins, Minnesota. Coach Geno Auriemma explained that he couldn't commit to both star players. "We made the decision we thought we needed to make," he said.

Clark jumps for the shot in a game against her former dream college, Uconn.

Clark focuses on her game.

CHAPTER TWO:

Home State Hero

As a senior at Dowling Catholic High School, Clark had averaged 33.4 points, eight rebounds, four assists and 2.7 steals per game. She was also invited to play in two prestigious high school all-star games—the McDonald's All-American Game and the Jordan Brand Classic. But both were canceled because of the ongoing COVID-19 pandemic, which began in the spring of 2020. It was disappointing, but in the end, she could only be proud of her accomplishments. Clark finished her high school career with 2,547 points and 283 three-pointers.

Her first year at the University of Iowa was also impacted by the pandemic. In-person classes were moved online at the end of her first semester, and only select family members and friends were able to attend her basketball games. But the hushed atmosphere in the arenas didn't quiet Clark's competitive spirit.

IOWA
22
BIG
HAWKEYES

ZOOM IN: A QUIET SEASON

Carver-Hawkeye Arena has capacity for 14,498 fans—and it is often quite full of black-and-gold-clad spectators. But during the 2020–21 basketball season, when COVID precautions were in place, the building was noticeably empty. Clark and the Hawkeyes played for home crowds of 365 fans or fewer. At other college basketball arenas around the country, attendance restrictions were even tighter. The Hawkeyes played eight regular-season games with no audience at all. Although the Big Ten Tournament welcomed more fans (1,202 people watched Iowa lose to Maryland in the title game), the NCAA tournament that followed was played without any fans in attendance.

Clark does not let her quick fame in the basketball world affect her game.

The six-foot point guard confidently entered the court at Carver-Hawkeye Arena in Iowa City for the Hawkeye's first game on November 25, 2020. She scored 27 points that night, grabbing eight rebounds and tallying four assists as the Hawkeyes cruised to a 96–81 win over the University of Northern Iowa.

In the next game, Clark posted a double-double—racking up double digits in both points (30) and assists (13). A few weeks later, she finished with a triple double: 13 points, 13 rebounds and 10 assists. By the end of the season, she had tallied the most points (799) of any women's college basketball player in the nation. She was also top in the United States in assists (214), points per game (26.6), three-pointers attempted (286) and three-pointers made (116).

Clark, who started in all 30 games in the 2020–21 season, quickly became a team leader. She and sophomore forward Monika Czinano formed a powerful duo that could consistently put the ball in the hoop and help the Hawkeyes win games. During the season, Christy Winters-Scott, an analyst with the Big Ten Network, gave them the nickname "The Law Firm of Clark and Czinano." Soon, the two were known simply as "The Law Firm."

Together, they led the Hawkeyes to a 2010 regular season record and into the Sweet 16 round of the National Collegiate Athletic Association (NCAA) tournament. There, they faced the

UConn Huskies and Bueckers, the freshman **phenom** who was also having an amazing season. Clark scored 21 points—three more than Bueckers, who netted 18. But the Huskies came out on top, 92–72, and Bueckers was named the national Player of the Year.

Clark earned her share of honors as well. She was the Big 10 Player of the Week five times—a record for a first-year student. She was also the first Big 10 freshman to be honored as an ESPN National Player of the Week. She was the first freshman to receive the Dawn Staley Award as the best all-around guard in DI women's basketball. When Staley, the head coach of the South Carolina women's basketball team, presented the award, she said, "Caitlin is going to be a huge part of women's basketball for a long time."

Clark's sophomore season confirmed Staley's statement. She again led the nation in several categories, including points per game (27) and assists per game (eight). She had five triple-doubles during the season, including two back-to-back triple-doubles with 30 points each. In doing so, she joined an elite group of basketball players—including such stars as LeBron James and Kobe Bryant—who had done so since 2000.

But what set her apart even from those players—and sparked comparisons to NBA great Steph Curry—was her ability to hit three-point shots. She had started sharpening that skill with extra hours in the gym after not being selected for Team USA's U-17 team in high school. Her parents even expanded the concrete in their driveway so she could practice long shots at regulation distance. All of that work came together at Iowa, where she found her sweet spot just

Clark's signature "number 3" has become an anticipated move when she successfully makes long shots.

IOWA
22

shy of the Hawkeye logo at half-court. Fans loved to watch her make deep jump shots from the edge of the logo, no matter what court she was playing on.

On February 6, 2022, Clark sank three of those deep shots with her feet in the blue paint of Michigan's block-M logo at the Crisler Center in Ann Arbor, Michigan. Although Iowa lost that game, Clark scored 25 points in the fourth quarter, including four three-pointers, to get the Hawkeyes within eight points of the Wolverines. The video of her performance—and of the stunned television announcer asking, "What did she just do?"—went viral.

As Clark's **notoriety** grew, so did the hopes of the Hawkeyes. The team ended the regular season with a 24–8 overall record and shared the Big Ten conference title with Ohio State. After topping Indiana 74–67 to win the Big Ten tournament title, Clark and the team were optimistic heading into the NCAA tournament. But instead of making it to the fabled Final Four, the Hawkeyes were eliminated in the second round by Creighton University.

Clark was honored as the Big Ten Player of the Year and the Most Valuable Player of the Big Ten Tournament. She was named

ZOOM IN: COACH LISA BLUDER

Lisa Bluder was introduced as the head coach of the Iowa Hawkeyes women's basketball team on April 7, 2000—two years before Clark was born. She had already spent six years coaching at St. Ambrose University in Davenport, Iowa and 10 at Drake University in Des Moines. But at Iowa, she stayed for 24 years and became the all-time winningest coach in program history. Bluder led the Hawkeyes to two NCAA national championship games, in 2023 and 2024. On May 13, 2024, shortly after losing to South Carolina in the title game, Bluder announced her retirement.

Iowa Hawkeyes coach Lisa Bluder.

the Nancy Lieberman Point Guard of the Year and became the first person to win the Dawn Staley Guard of the Year Award in consecutive seasons. The marketing major also made the Dean's List and earned Academic All-Big Ten Honors.

None of that dulled Clark's disappointment of the early loss in the tournament. But it did stoke the fire burning in her belly. As Clark prepared for her junior year, she had her sights set on reaching the Final Four.

Wilson
LSU TIGERS
IOWA
22
LSU
45
2

CHAPTER THREE:

Championship Buzz

During the offseason between her sophomore and junior seasons, Clark's older brother Blake would occasionally send her the same text. It was a picture of the scoreboard he'd taken when Iowa lost to Creighton at the end of the 2022 season. He knew the sight of that score would motivate his sister.

Not that Clark needed extra inspiration. She started her junior season knowing that it would be her last opportunity to win a championship with teammates Czinano and McKenna Warnock, whom she had played with for the previous two years. She had been heralded as a preseason favorite to top both the Big 10 and the NCAA. And she had earned a national reputation for making big plays—especially three-pointers—in important games.

But Clark was still also battling the reputation about her expressive body language. She alternatively appeared to be over celebratory about her success and overly frustrated about what she saw as bad calls, misplays by teammates, and aggressive opponents.

Clark is renowned for her accuracy and composure on the court.

ZOOM IN: THE 2024 OLYMPIC TEAM

When the 12-person roster for Team USA women's basketball was announced on June 9, 2024, the one name that was conspicuously not on the list was Clark's. Many outside observers had assumed that she would be a shoo-in for a spot. But the decision-making process was much more complicated. Some of those involved said they had to consider her current standing in the WNBA more than her previous successes and that she didn't meet the selection criteria. Although the decision was widely criticized, Clark herself said she wasn't disappointed and that she would be cheering on the team.

Coach Bluder and her staff continued to work with Clark on managing her demeanor on the court. They compiled a clip file and regularly showed her video of her reactions during practices and games. When they could point out a positive reaction—walking off the court during practice instead of throwing her water bottle or slamming a chair, for example—they would talk through why it was a good choice.

Those lessons were crucial when the Hawkeyes lost three key games early in the season. But Clark got hot in December and the team rebounded to win six straight games. In one of the games, against Dartmouth, Clark passed the 2,000-point mark. Clark reached that milestone in just 75 games, tying Elena Delle Donne, who played for the Delaware Blue Hens from 2009 to

Clark celebrates a win during March Madness (2023).

LSU
10
IOWA
22

Clark's rival Angel Reese gestures to her after their heated game.

2013, as the fastest to reach 2,000 points. By the end of the season, the Hawkeyes had compiled a 31–7 record with only one loss at home. And, after winning their second consecutive Big Ten Tournament title, the Hawkeyes went back to the NCAA Tournament favored to win.

Finally, Clark made good on her promise to take the Hawkeyes back to the Final Four for the first time since 1993. Once there, she was determined to get to the championship game. Clark scored 41 points in the **penultimate** game against South Carolina, leading Iowa to a 77–73 victory and a **berth** in the final game of the tournament.

The Hawkeyes faced off against the Louisiana State University Tigers and their star player, Angel Reese. It wasn't even close. The more athletic Tigers won easily, 102–85, but Clark tallied the most points (20) in the game and came away with a new **nemesis**. As equally passionate and competitive players, she and Reese played hard against each other and engaged in some back-and-forth chatter and hand gestures during the game. Because the nationally televised game was watched by as many as 12.6 million viewers, their **rivalry** became big news.

Thanks to that national attention, Clark and the Hawkeyes were the hot ticket during the 2023–24 season. In August, the University of Iowa Athletics Department announced that for the first time ever, the women's basketball program had sold out of season tickets. Even at away games, arenas were selling more tickets when Clark came to town. Of the 39 total games they played that season, 37 either set an attendance record or sold out—or both.

Almost always in attendance at those games were Clark's mom and dad, and often one or both of her brothers. It became an endearing tradition for Clark to make a heart with her hands and hold it up toward her family in the stands at the end of a game. Her mom and dad were often shown during televised games. They shouted encouragement or cheered wildly for their daughter. And the star player always tried to greet them in person at the end of the game as well.

During her senior season, they witnessed several remarkable moments—including Clark breaking several records. Clark had entered the season just 810 points shy of the all-time NCAA Division I women's scoring record, and 950 points away from Pete Maravich's record for most points in Division I basketball history—a record that had stood for 54 years. Clark broke the first record with a from-the-logo three-pointer in Carver-Hawkeye Arena on February 15, 2024. The second fell during her last regular season home game, when she sank two free-throws just before the end of the first half to set the new record.

That game was an emotional rollercoaster for Clark and her family, and not just because of the broken record. Earlier that week, Clark had announced her decision not to play a fifth season at Iowa, which was possible because of the COVID-19 pandemic. Instead, she planned to enter the Women's National Basketball Association (WNBA) **draft** after the season ended.

But Clark and her teammates were focused on the season ahead. They had their sights set on returning to the Final Four—and

ZOOM IN: ANGEL OR DEVIL?

Most fans first saw Clark and Reese spar on the court during the national championship game in 2023. But the two star basketball players had actually known each other since competing on different AAU teams in junior high and high school. And although their behavior during games may have made it seem like they disliked each other, the two actually share mutual respect and admiration. Both have publicly said that they harbor no ill will or hard feelings toward the other. "It's just basketball," Reese said in an interview in 2024. "It gets crazy sometimes."

Clark is noted for her maturity on and off the court.

WNBA
PRADA

ZOOM IN: SWOOSH SUPPORT

In the spring of 2024, as Clark broke scoring records and the Hawkeyes were heading toward the NCAA tournament, billboards featuring quotes about her started popping up around Iowa City. The simple billboards were put up by Nike, which had signed a Name, Image, Likeness (NIL) sponsorship agreement with Clark in 2022. Nike also installed two giant signs on two different buildings. The first showed Clark shooting one of her signature three-pointers. The second was a giant hoop with the words "This was never a long shot." The billboards and signs went viral and were widely praised for their support of women's sports and female athletes.

also to the championship game. To get there, they had to face Louisiana State University in the Elite Eight matchup. This time, it was a much closer game—and this time, Iowa came out on top, beating the Tigers 94–87 to make their second consecutive trip to the Final Four.

In the first game, the Hawkeyes narrowly defeated UConn—and Bueckers—71–69. That meant they would have to face South Carolina, which had been undefeated in the regular season, in the title game. Although the Hawkeyes came out hot and quickly took a 10–0 lead, South Carolina eventually overpowered them and ended up winning 87–75.

During her four years at Iowa, Clark compiled 3,951 total points, 1,144 assists, and 990 rebounds. She broke almost every record possible and received every honor available to a college basketball player. The only thing missing from her storied college career was a championship trophy.

CLARK
22

CHAPTER FOUR:

Fever Pitch

Clark's college basketball career ended after the national championship game on April 7, 2024—but the rest of her life was just beginning. She was a month away from graduating with a bachelor's degree in marketing from the University of Iowa's Tippie College of Business, and only a week away from the WNBA draft, where she would be one of dozens of athletes selected by the 12 professional women's basketball teams.

But before any of that, Clark and her teammates returned to Carver-Hawkeye Arena to celebrate the season with fans. After learning that her number 22 jersey would be retired by the Hawkeyes, she traveled to Los Angeles for an annual awards ceremony, where she was named the National Player of the Year.

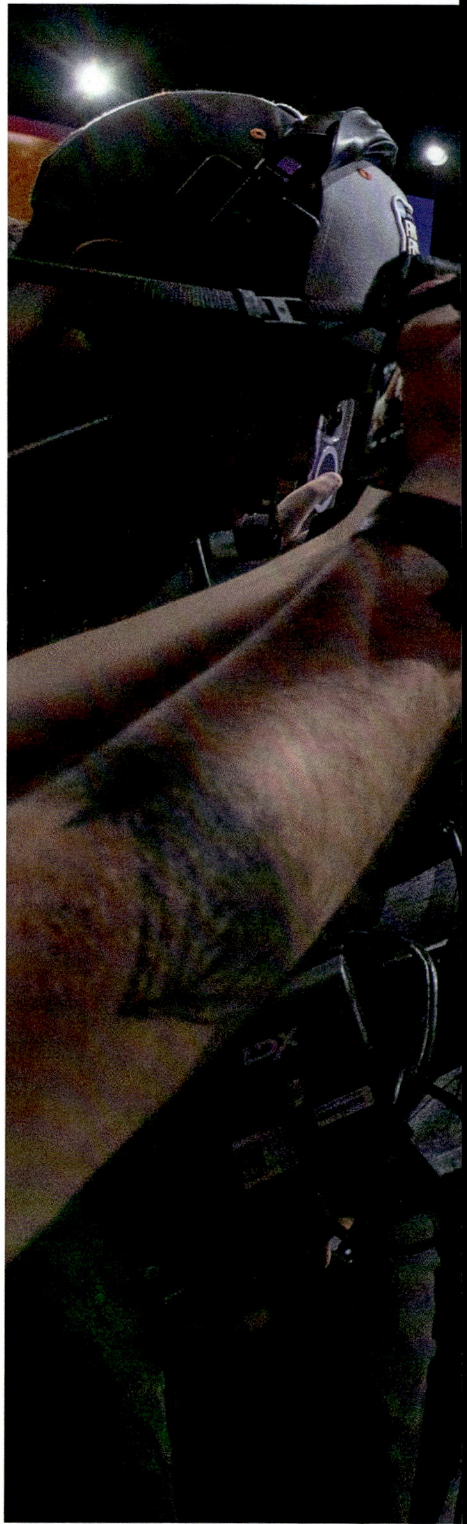

Clark at the 2024 WNBA draft.

ZOOM IN: ROOKIE OF THE YEAR

Clark's first year in the WNBA certainly had its struggles, but the star player still did what she does best. She started in all 40 of the Fever's regular-season games, became the first rookie in WNBA history to record a triple-double, and set a league record for the most assists in a game with 19. So when it was time for the panel of national sportswriters and broadcasters to vote for the Rookie of the Year after the 2024 season, 66 of the 67 votes cast were for Clark. The one vote not for Clark was for Reese, her former college rival.

Her next flight took her to New York City, where the draft would take place on Monday morning. But first, she made a cameo appearance on *Saturday Night Live,* joking about women's basketball with Michael Che on the show's Weekend Update segment.

On Monday, April 15, Clark arrived at the Empire State Building by 9 a.m. for the draft. Her national popularity had extended to that event as well. Fans were waiting for her to arrive wearing 22 jerseys, and more than 2.4 million viewers were watching on ESPN alone—up 328 percent over the previous year's draft. Almost everyone watching—either on TV or in person—knew what was going to happen when the league's commissioner, Cathy Engelbert, stepped to the microphone to announce the first pick of the draft.

Clark had been predicted to be the top overall pick in the draft by several media organizations, including ESPN, *USA Today* and CBS Sports. But even so, she was anxious as she sat at a table with her mom, dad and brothers, waiting for Engelbert to approach the podium. When she finally appeared, no one was surprised by what she said: "With the first pick in the 2024 WNBA Draft, the Indiana Fever select Caitlin Clark."

Clark's focus and skill continues, no matter what team she plays on.

In an interview immediately after the selection, Clark said she'd been dreaming of that moment since she was in second grade. "It's taken a lot of hard work, a lot of ups and downs," she said. "I'm just trying to soak it in."

But there wasn't much time for that. After celebrating with her family and friends, Clark flew to Indianapolis for a press conference with her new team. Then she returned to Iowa to wrap up her studies before starting training camp at the end of the month. Her schedule was so packed that she wasn't able to participate in her graduation ceremony on May 12, 2024. Clark, who graduated with a 3.64 GPA, was preparing for the Fever's first game of the season when her classmates were picking up their diplomas. But her new teammates didn't want her to miss out, so they coordinated an impromptu celebration and presented her with a Certificate of Graduation before practice started.

The Fever opened their season against the Connecticut Sun on May 14. Clark's first professional game didn't go well: she scored 20 points, but in the face of constant pressure by her opponents, she also turned the ball over 10 times. The Fever lost their first five games, and Clark took several hard hits in the process. It was a difficult introduction to the more physical game played at the professional level, but Fever head coach Christie Sides encouraged her 22-year-old star to be patient.

The first half of the season required a lot of patience for Clark, who was used to winning more games than she lost. Her team won only one of its first eight games

and had an 11–15 record in the middle of the season. But in terms of national attention, the Fever were a huge success. Almost all of their regular-season games were scheduled to be nationally televised. Sell-out crowds were packing into Gainbridge Fieldhouse, where they played their home games, and prominent companies such as Cheez-Its and Salesforce had signed up to become jersey sponsors. Clark herself was inking a long list of **endorsement** deals as well, including Nike, Gatorade, State Farm and Xfinity.

The team was eager for the break afforded by the 2024 Summer Olympic Games. Although Clark was disappointed to be left off Team USA, she had been actively competing for almost a full year and was tired. She participated in the All-Star Weekend activities (she had received more than 700,000 votes from fans, the most of any player in the league). Then she spent the rest of the time working on her game with the coaches, playing golf and watching a New York Yankees baseball game.

Clark, who graduated with a 3.64 GPA, was preparing for the Fever's first game of the season when her classmates were picking up their diplomas.

After the break, the Fever went 5–1 in August and won their first two games in September—which earned them a place in the playoffs for the first time in seven years. The team finished the season with a respectable 20–20 record. Clark finished the season ranked first

in the league with three-pointers (122) and assists per game (8.4). She was also tops among all **rookies** in points scored, field goals, steals per game and free-throw percentage.

Although the Fever were swept in the first round of the 2024 playoffs by Connecticut, the team was building momentum for the future. And so was Clark. She was honored as Rookie of the Year and was the fifth rookie in WNBA history to be named to the All-WNBA First Team. But she is only getting started. With her competitive spirit and determination to be the best, Clark will continue to make big plays, orchestrate wins and break records in the WNBA.

Highlight Reels

FROM THE LOGO

During the course of her college career, Clark became known not only as a prolific and proficient three-point shooter, but also for the distance from which she could sink shots. The three-point line in college basketball—for both men and women—is 22 feet and 1.75 inches (6.7 m, 4.44 centimeters) from the center of the basket. But Clark didn't often get that close to shoot.

Sportswriters and broadcasters started using the phrase "from the logo" to describe her deep shots; her feet were often still in or near the painted college logo when she put the shot up. At Carver-Hawkeye Arena in Iowa City, Clark made it a habit to be within or near the black-and-gold-painted Hawkeye logo when she shot.

Her longest three-pointer came on February 16, 2024 in a game against Michigan. She put the shot up from the edge of the Hawkeye logo—a full 35 feet (10.6 m) from the basket. That shot was not only her longest, it also tallied the final three points she needed to break the all-time NCAA women's basketball scoring record.

Her three-point game has remained strong as she's moved to professional basketball. As of August 2024, the average distance of Clark's three-pointers in the WNBA was 28.09 feet (8.56 m). That's longer than the career bests of such NBA sharpshooters as Steph Curry, Damian Lilliard, and Trae Young. And during her time with the Fever, her three-point shooting percentage—which is the number of successful shots divided by total attempted shots—gets higher the farther back she goes.

GROWING THE GAME

Clark recognizes the role she plays in advancing women's basketball, and women's sports in general. She knows that the attention she's received has brought unprecedented attention to the game—and she hopes that will continue even after she's done playing.

In a postgame press conference after beating Indiana in the last regular season game of the 2023 season, Clark was asked what it meant to play such a big game with so many young girls watching in the stands and on television.

"I'm all about growing the women's game," she said. "I'm glad I've given something that little girls can scream about at the top of their lungs. I can imagine when I was younger, I was doing the exact same thing watching on TV. It's pretty fun."

Clark's impact on the game went well beyond the sold-out stands at Iowa's Carver-Hawkeye Arena. The NCAA reported that a total of 292,456 fans attended the first- and second-round games of the 2024 women's NCAA tournament. That's an increase of more than 60,000 fans than in 2023. In 2019, before Clark started playing for the Hawkeyes, a total of 274,873 fans attended the entire women's NCAA tournament.

With so many accolades to her name, her most important legacy may be the additional attention she's brought to women's basketball and the next generation of girls she's inspired.

HEART IN HER HANDS

Clark isn't the first person to make a heart by curling her fingers, pointing her thumbs down and joining her hands. It's a gesture that's been made popular by dozens of young celebrities, including singers Justin Bieber, Selena Gomez, and Demi Lovato. A corresponding emoji is often even shared on texts and social media posts. But Clark has become known for making heart hands after games.

The heart-shaped hands are used to convey feelings of love and gratitude, often to a large group of people. In Clark's case, she uses the simple gesture to send a message of love to her family after a game and to say thanks to all the fans who've come out to support her. Photos and videos from dozens of Iowa Hawkeye games show the star player looking into the crowd with her hands shaped in a heart. Often, she held her hands close to her heart and smiled up at the stands. On the night of her last game played at Carver-Hawkeye Arena, she raised her arms above her head, quickly pumped her fists, and then made her signature heart hands as a final thank-you and farewell to the Iowa fans.

The simple gesture has become a signature move for Clark and has followed her from college to the pros. It has been memorialized on merchandise, including trading cards and t-shirts. And fans often make heart hands in the stands to show their love and appreciation for Clark as well.

Glossary

amateur—non-professional sports competition

berth—a spot that allows a team to participate in post-season events like tournaments

capacity—the maximum number of people a building can hold

criteria—a standard or set of standards by which decisions are made

demeanor—outward behavior

draft—a system of selecting athletes to be part of professional teams

endorsement—when an athlete gets paid to promote certain products or services

nemesis—a rival

NCAA—National Collegiate Athletic Association; the organization responsible for organizing sports competitions between universities in the United States

notoriety—being widely known

parabola—a symmetrical, u-shaped curve

penultimate—the second to last event in a series

phenom—an extremely talented person who is an up-and-coming star in their field

point guard—the player on a basketball team responsible for bringing the ball up the court and setting up the offensive plays

rivalry—two parties who compete fiercely for the same goal

rookie—in sports, an athlete who is in their first year of playing in a league

tournament—a series of competitions between a number of teams all competing for an overall prize

varsity—the main competitive team representing a specific high school or college

Selected Bibliography

"Caitlin Clark, American Icon," *Athlon Sports*, A360Media, Englewood Cliffs, New Jersey. 2024.

"Caitlin Clark, Basketball's Best," *ESPN*, Meredith Premium Publishing, New York. 2024.

"Caitlin Clark: Raising the Game," *The Athletic*, Triumph Books, Chicago. 2024.

Iowa Hawkeyes Roster: Caitlin Clark. https://hawkeyesports.com/roster/caitlin-clark/, December 4, 2024.

Websites

Indiana Fever
https://fever.wnba.com/
Learn more about Caitlin Clark and her team.

WNBA
https://www.wnba.com
Learn about the professional women's basketball league.

Kids Encyclopedia
https://kids.kiddle.co/Caitlin_Clark
Find out more about Caitlin Clark.

Index